Restoring a Dunkirk Little Ship: Caronia SS70

PETER DRAPER

AMBERLEY

I dedicate this book to the 'Dunkirk Spirit' – the steadfast determination to not give up on something just because it appears too hard or in some cases nearly impossible – and to the men on the beaches who believed somehow they would get home and to the men and women who had the guts and spirit to do all they could to bring them back. It was in their memories and with their spirit I undertook the task of rebuilding Caronia. *I would like to think that my determination has inspired my own children to strive for and achieve their own voyages, Natalie with her Master's degree and Lewis with his career as a Merchant Navy engineer. I hope this book inspires others to seek out these famous and historic craft, as by keeping them afloat they also keep that spirit of 1940 alive.*

First published 2017

Amberley Publishing
The Hill, Stroud,
Gloucestershire, GL5 4EP

www.amberley-books.com

Copyright © Peter Draper, 2017

The right of Peter Draper to be identified as the Author
of this work has been asserted in accordance with the
Copyrights, Designs and Patents Act 1988.

All rights reserved. No part of this book may be reprinted
or reproduced or utilised in any form or by any electronic,
mechanical or other means, now known or hereafter invented,
including photocopying and recording, or in any information
storage or retrieval system, without the permission in writing
from the Publishers.

ISBN 978 1 4456 7558 9 (print)
ISBN 978 1 4456 7559 6 (ebook)

British Library Cataloguing in Publication Data.
A catalogue record for this book is available from the British Library.

Typeset in 10pt on 13pt Celeste.
Origination by Amberley Publishing.
Printed in the UK.

Contents

Introduction

Restore, rebuild or repair. Which one is the most applicable to your project is a matter of opinion and conjecture. If you ever take on your own project on the scale of *Caronia* it will be something you will be asked and will ask yourself many times: am I restoring the original item or simply replicating what was built many years ago?

Obviously, when it comes to a wooden boat, especially one the age of *Caronia*, if you want to keep the vessel seaworthy then rotten planking and rusted fittings have to be replaced and refurbished. Planks and frames ravaged by worm, wet or dry rot have to come out and serviceable repairs made. That's the way I like to think of it: I am not replacing or replicating, I am repairing, no different to an old car on the London to Brighton run sporting new tyres fitted last week, otherwise it wouldn't be on the road.

So it is with *Caronia*. The engine is not original, as in it is not the one fitted in 1927; it couldn't be – it would be totally worn out and unserviceable. It is, however, a suitable marine diesel engine fit for purpose and up to the job of propelling *Caronia*'s considerable tonnage. The same is true of the planks that were replaced due to damage by worm or the new wheelhouse which replaced the unsuitable and poorly constructed previous deck shelter. I am, however, glad to say that the majority of *Caronia*'s original hull is very much still the same wood that was fastened together by hand tools and ship nails on a Cornish beach over nine decades ago. Undertaking a restoration project of any kind, whether vehicle or vessel, should not be considered lightly. If you just don't have the skills or the time then it would be foolish to believe it's ever going to be anything other than a very expensively paid for stand-and-watch process or you may end up with a large heap of disassembled parts listed for sale under the auctions site heading of 'project'.

Utilising paid skilled labour will still get the job done but it's never going to give the same sense of achievement as completing it yourself. I am fortunate to have spent the majority of my life as an engineer and worked with metal and wood. During *Caronia*'s rebuild I had to learn new skills and conquer new challenges. It was hard work and more than once I considered just giving up, but I didn't. The adventures and time *Caronia* has given me with my family along with the award this year of National Historic Flagship have made it all worthwhile. I will freely admit, though, that it was very hard work.

Above: *Caronia*, restored, rebuilt and repaired to a fully seaworthy vessel, at sea in 2016 on the passage to Dunkirk. Thanks to Geoff Turner for this and the cover photo.

Left: What it was all for. At sea on a calm summer's early morning, enjoying a smooth passage towards home.

The ultimate recognition of all the years of hard work. With Lewis at the presentation of the National Historic Ships Flagship award, and with Natalie as we hoisted the pennant on the mainmast.

Caronia was built on the beach at Tolcarne, Newlyn, Cornwall, by Henry, Theodore and Sidney Peake. In 1927 her keel was laid for Mike Peters, a fishing boat skipper from St Ives. Her hull was in the form of a traditional St Ives Gig and she proudly wore SS70, the fishing license registration mark of a St Ives-based vessel.

Launched over greased spars, she was then towed round into the harbour to have her engines fitted, a 26 hp Kelvin in the center and a 13 hp on the port wing. The machinery was fitted by Tresidders of St Ives and the costs of the build were split between Mike Peters and his brother James. Mike paid for the hull and James picked up the bill for the engines. *Caronia* cost a princely £180 to build in a year when the average house price was £410.

The beach in Newlyn where we believe *Caronia* may have been built back in 1927. It is still in use today for the maintenance of Cornish boats.

A recent rebuild of a vessel carrying the St Ives SS registration, this photo could be two or eighty years old – the beach hasn't changed, nor its usefulness for such work.

A very early picture, believed to be at St Ives and taken in 1933. Her SS70 registration can be clearly seen. This shows how she started life as an open boat.

She was one of the very first of her line to have engines as her primary power source rather than sails. These seemingly low-power engines were not intended to drive her directly but to keep large heavy flywheels spinning, and their kinetic energy drove the shaft and propellers. The engines also explain her flat transom – her earlier sisters had a counter stern to give space to work the larger mizzen sail. The shorter overall length also kept her in a cheaper fishing licence category.

Her gig hull was completed with tiller steering and a mizzen lug sail. She didn't steam home to St Ives her first year but remained at Newlyn for the summer's pilchard drifting. This was known as 'going to the Wolf', as the majority of the large pilchard shoals were to be found out close to the Wolf Rock. Her first season was such a success that she repaid her build cost with the profitable catch. Soon after this she was raised and fitted with a gaff mizzen and wheelhouse. It was from this time in Cornish waters that a tale stems that she undertook her first act of mercy by coming to the assistance of a foundering passenger liner.

Now looking more like a gentleman's motorboat, *Caronia* is seen following her conversion at Littlehampton in 1933. Thanks to Mark Dilbert for this photo.

By 1934 the fishing at St Ives was in a poor state and the fishing fleet was dispersing to find other incomes. *Caronia* was sold to Mr Bennet Burley, a solicitor based in London, who had a holiday residence in River Road, Littlehampton, West Sussex. Mike Peters sailed *Caronia* to her new home and moored her at Osbourne's yard. Her new owner employed his own carpenter to convert her into a motor yacht under Mike Peters's supervision and guidance. Over the next two years she took on her new guise and when work was completed she more resembled a gentleman's launch rather than a fishing boat. The net and fish rooms were converted into a saloon and a toilet, bunks were fitted in the forepeak and the fisherman's wheelhouse was converted into a more cruiser style.

In May 1940 the violence of war in Europe changed who *Caronia* was and what she would be known for throughout the rest of history. At the outbreak of the Second World War *Caronia* was in Le Havre, requiring a hurried return to Newhaven where she was commandeered by the navy and in the company of many hundreds of other Little Ships she steamed to the beaches of Dunkirk. It is believed she stayed with the navy for the rest of the war before being released back into private use.

Over the years we have collected many books on the story of Dunkirk, one of which was written in November 1940, only six months after the event and *Caronia*'s participation. It has her listed in the pages and pages of vessels large and small, each with its own story to tell, each of those vessels crewed by brave men, in some cases by their owners and volunteer civilian crews.

Troops on the beaches of Dunkirk. Estimates vary but at any one time it is believed that as many as half a million soldiers and civilians were waiting to be rescued.

Troops wading out to one of the many hundreds of ships used to ferry survivors out to larger vessels or make their own passage across the Channel.

A lot of the smaller vessels were towed en masse to the beaches by larger ships to act as ferry boats, taking war-weary men out to the larger vessels offshore. Some scurried to and fro across the Channel carrying as many survivors as possible. Fishing boats, ferry boats, day trippers, private craft and river cruisers. The requisition was for vessels over 30 feet, but many smaller craft made the journey and many never returned.

I will continue to research her time spent in those frantic, dreadful days between 26 May and 4 June 1940 but in some cases the records from which the subsequent accounts were made have been lost and the names of some vessels and crews were never recorded. We do have enough evidence to prove *Caronia* can proudly be known by history as a 'Dunkirk Little Ship'. Evidence found so far leads us to believe she made the passage to and fro between Dunkirk and home shores under her own power with rescued troops aboard.

After the war *Caronia* returned to use as a pleasure yacht on the South Coast of England. By the mid-1960s she had reverted to her original use as a fishing vessel engaged in trawling from Brightlingsea. It was during this time that she saw action again, but this time on the wrong side of the law. She and her master got into trouble with the authorities for running supplies out to *Mi Amigo*, Radio Caroline. In the eyes of the law she was smuggling, although on the east coast her Cornish heritage may have played a part in this mischief.

Caronia then underwent a further conversion to a pleasure yacht in the 1970s at Pin Mill and for the next twenty or so years she ranged between pleasure use and fishing. She spent time in Grimsby and steamed from the harbour of Torquay to fish for sharks.

Above: *Caronia* back in private use after the war and enjoying a more tranquil setting. Thanks to Mark Dilbert for this photo.

Left: Fans on their way out to Radio Caroline to meet the DJs sometime in the early 1970s. Thanks to Nick Catford for this and the other Radio Caroline photos.

Right: *Caronia*, licenced to carry twelve persons, showing that she was taking a break from fishing to earn her living carrying passengers.

Below: A warning notice to boat owners, obviously ignored by the then skipper.

WARNING
TO BOAT OWNERS
It is illegal to carry
goods or persons to or from
PIRATE
BROADCASTING
STATIONS

Left: Steaming out of Shoreham in the late 1980s, now with a fisherman's wheelhouse.

Below: As we first saw her, in yet another colour scheme and wheelhouse design, on the eastern arm of Brighton Marina.

By the mid-1990s she was starting to feel her age and was in Shoreham in generally poor condition. She was rescued by the owner before us, who did enough to keep her afloat and converted her to a full time live-aboard.

He had not long had it confirmed that she was indeed a Little Ship when I purchased her in 2002. The knowledge that she had taken part in such a significant event in history fascinated and intrigued me and although it was not the entire reason I took ownership, it did influence my final decision.

1

A New Home

We sailed *Caronia* from her mooring in Brighton Marina, where she had resided for eleven years, to Birdham Pool in the beautiful setting of Chichester Harbour, where she lived happily attending various events. She was used as a base for family adventures and special days, including a full Christmas dinner cooked on the small two-burner oven. The interior fit-out was warm and cosy, the bunks were comfortable and to be honest, for some time I would just take my daughter Natalie and son Lewis to her every weekend. Their lives became entwined with *Caronia* and Natalie had her first published article printed on the memories of the day they first went aboard. Lewis, after years of learning engineering skills during the restoration, is now a Merchant Navy engineer.

Sometimes on our days aboard *Caronia* we went for short runs down the harbour; sometimes we cooked and ate on board and sat in front of the temperamental old brass diesel-fired heater. In summer we barbequed on the bank and the children rowed the inflatable dingy around the enclosed waters of Birdham Pool. *Caronia* was our den; it was for some time an idyllic way to spend time with the children. The addition of ship's dog Wilson completed the crew when he was eleven weeks old. Wilson, named after the volleyball in the Tom Hanks film *Castaway*, is still with me now, hundreds of sea miles under his paws, as white-whiskered as a true old pirate and laying at my feet in the wheelhouse as I type this.

This book is going to take you through the major projects that were required to take *Caronia* from a very comfortable, afloat live-aboard to the proud vessel that has attended some significant events such as the Diamond Jubilee Pageant, Dunkirk returns and the filming of the Warner Brothers epic *Dunkirk*. Every project, every job, was undertaken by the author and son Lewis with some painting by daughter Natalie when she was home from university plus a few weeks' extra help from an old shipwright.

Unfortunately, the first time I went to sea as skipper of *Caronia* for the voyage to her new home port, restoration was the last thing on my mind. We set out from Brighton at first light and had been at sea for less than a couple of hours. Just off Littlehampton the gearbox drive plate sheared. An unceremonious tow took us back to Shoreham behind the all-weather lifeboat. This was only *Caronia*'s third venture off her mooring in eleven years and it was a poor example of her true worth.

I knew when I paid for *Caronia* that there was going to be a lot of work to do to make her completely seaworthy again, but I had hoped we would at least get her to her new mooring in Birdham before I had to start the work. So long before we had to consider renovation or restoration, it was a case of straightforward repair. The gearbox was out by the same afternoon, a quick strip and check, a new drive plate and on our way again to Birdham a couple of days later. There was absolutely no doubt in my mind that the first job was going to be to source, purchase and fit a new engine or at least, as it turned out, an engine that would last us a few years until the piggy bank could run to a new unit.

In 2002 it was a bit before the now much-used internet auction sites got going. It was a case of searching all the boating publications and tracking down breakers and firms who dealt in old boat parts. I found a dealer in Kent who had a Leyland Terrier 5.66, a straight six-cylinder engine that had seen a fair life's work in a Thames workboat. I rented a van and had a family day out to go and collect it.

The actual fitting of the Leyland was pretty straight forward; it was to sit in the same location as the current 3.4 BMC and connect to the same shaft. I made an engine bed template to get the angles and spacings, then made a new pair of beds and bearers. I always knew that this engine would be a temporary measure until the final power plant was dropped in. So the engine beds were up to the job but nothing like the ones later built for the new engine to come. The wheelhouse, if you could stretch to that description for the garden shed in place of where the future wheelhouse would go, was modified with the aid of a power saw and off came the roof.

The stripped out and completely underpowered little 3.4 BMC, now heading for the scrapyard.

The Leyland was swung under the old naval crane at Birdham Pool (sadly the crane was taken out recently as part of the refurbishment of the yard) and gently dropped onto the engine beds. As we had the roof off anyway, we also craned in a BMC 1500, which was destined to be the port wing engine, giving *Caronia* back her original engine configuration of main and wing. In her life as a pilchard seine-netter, the main would have been used to steam out to the fishing grounds and the wing utilised to cast a long purse net around the pilchard shoals. I wanted the wing to add authenticity and for the obvious comfort of having a backup engine.

The Leyland being lifted by the old naval girder crane.

A very tight fit down the aft hatch into the engine room.

The little BMC had been sourced, like the Leyland, from the adverts in the back of the boating press. This time, though, I was pleased to see the STD code was a local number, the two digit prefix was my local area and the phone was answered by an old boy I had known from the local pub for many years. 'I didn't know you had a boat Percy,' I said. 'I don't, that's why I am selling the engine.' We named the BMC 'Percy' in his honour and we still know her as this. The big Leyland took on the title 'Peter', being both my name and the name of the chap we bought her from. The Leyland did us good service, taking *Caronia* to the Dunkirk Return in 2005, the fleet review for Trafalgar 200 and, not insignificantly, the 2012 Diamond Jubilee Pageant.

The Leyland 'Peter' and the BMC 1500 'Percy' sitting side by side in the engine room.

The gearbox connection to the old and somewhat undersized shaft.

The 2005 Dunkirk Return was an epic worthy of future telling, and the first sea trial of the Leyland. The weather was poor and we had a series of engine problems. We did manage to sail with the fleet out of Ramsgate but only arrived there late in the evening before we crossed to Dunkirk.

Leaving for the Dunkirk Return 2005. The wheelhouse roof has been repaired and has had a coat of paint to tidy it up.

At Ramsgate, the night before we crossed to Dunkirk, for *Caronia*'s first time back since the war.

In amongst the fleet in Dunkirk, looking a bit battle-worn and not at her best.

Early in 2006 we took on the task of replacing the shed wheelhouse; in fairness to the previous owner, the wheelhouse he had built had been intended as more of a conservatory than a shelter from which to helm a classic old fishing boat. A look around old harbours and leafing through various classic boat books led me to decide on the Cornish style of wheelhouse. Well, you can't get much more Cornish than a fishing boat from St Ives. Ironically, to replace the wheelhouse that looked like a shed, I built the new one, in sections, in my shed.

The new wheel shelter was built mainly from reclaimed and repurposed timber from demolished hardwood conservatories that I collected from a local double glazing manufacturer. Having a well-equipped home workshop is a must if you're going to take on a nearly ninety-year-old, 40-ton fishing boat. The final design was to be a hammer-head footprint with a standing height to the hammer, and a door either side; I like to be able to look directly at the sea when underway. A lower seating area forms the handle of the hammer with an L-shape seat around the hatchway to the aft space. The new wheelhouse was built in six sections. The aft lower was to surround the seats and aft upper had windows and a curved roof. This was the part that was removed some years later to allow the Leyland to come out and its replacement to go in. The front section had the roof and windows as one piece and the door frames made up sections five and six. I must have got something right as another wooden boat enthusiast has just come to measure up to build a copy for the old pilot cutter he is restoring.

The new wheelhouse as it still looks today, and still giving good service. A door is on either side for easy access.

The aft section, which has seating and allows the upper section with the windows to be removed for major maintenance projects.

On the day of the new wheelhouse fit *Caronia* was again moved to the work area of Birdham Pool and without too much dignity the old pine-slatted, flat-roofed shed was removed. I think the hardest part was cutting through the repairs we had done after putting the Leyland in a year or so previously. The new wheelhouse had been transported down on a borrowed trailer after the slightly comical process of removing half the side section of my workshop to allow the prefabricated new woodwork to be removed.

It was a simple matter of literally clearing the deck and putting the new sections in place, bolting them down and together and then constructing what was in effect section seven, which was the lower front frame to join the windows to the coach roof. Fit the doors, seal the seams, coat of preservative on the hardwood and white paint on the roof and that was a major job done. Well, at that time I thought it was one of the major jobs we were ever likely to undertake on *Caronia*.

Caronia stayed pretty much unchanged for the next two years or more. The Leyland did all we wanted for little local trips; the new wheelhouse had the interior fitted out with instruments and seats and in the process the old chain steering was changed to hydraulics, allowing the wheel to be moved further forward and granting access to the portside door. We never liked the hydraulic steering; it had no feel and didn't make that lovely rattling noise as the chains dragged their way to the tiller. It was later to be changed back to the complex mechanical steering binnacle after an extensive rebuild. The interior of *Caronia* was very comfortable and she was ideal for her previous purpose as a live-aboard. But things were to change.

2

Rot and Repair

Early in 2008, while spending a weekend on board and enjoying the peaceful surroundings, something came to my attention, something which any boat owner dreads: the sound of running water, that is, water running into the boat. I remember it well. It was the weekend of the Beaulieu Boat Jumble that I had gone to for years to source bits for my previous boat. I spent the day instead in my old commercial diving gear with a sheet of copper and a handful of nails. I was basically nailing a big copper sticking plaster over what turned out to be a sprung plank. It had been weakened by the attention of Gribble worm, a nasty little blighter that bores along the grain of the wood so from the outside it may look sound but inside it's a weak honeycomb. This situation was not helped by someone having drilled a Blakes sea cock through the sickly plank. Blakes have a centre spigot and four surrounding bolts, so you need very sound woodwork to fit one into.

Making use of some old skills to do some much-needed emergency repairs.

The sprung plank had been dealt with by some undoubtedly frightened individual pouring in some fast-setting concrete to fill the space between the first three bow frames. This quick fix had now let go, hence the unpleasant sound of incoming water. It is said that the best bilge pump is a frightened man with a bucket; I think this one had a bucket and a cement mixer.

The tingle, as the repair patches are known, stood up well but it was apparent that some serious work was going to be needed. So in the summer of 2008 *Caronia* made the only passage she was going to make for some time across from Birdham Pool to Chichester Marina, where they had the space and the travel lift that could cope with *Caronia*'s 40 tons. The day we lifted out, my estimates of twelve to sixteen weeks to do all the work necessary to relaunch with a sound hull started to look a bit ambitious. As it turned out, grossly, colossally underestimated might be a better description.

In the doubled-up slings of Chichester Marina's travel lift. It was to be a very long time before she was back in those slings.

The work of the Gribble worm can clearly be seen and this is the port side, which was in better condition than the patched up starboard.

Sitting on the blocks in the corner of the boatyard, looking a little strange with a new wheelhouse but a damaged hull.

I had originally intended undertaking only the work required to get *Caronia* afloat again. That work was obvious; after the barnacles and weed had been scrapped away the extent of the bad planking was apparent. In fact, there were only four bow planks affected by the worm over no more than a 4-foot section. I suppose if the worm gets in a tasty plank, it stays there. Gribble can be found in slightly warmer water and *Caronia* had spent many years in Shoreham, where the power station outlet is known to keep the inner harbour slightly warmer than the surrounding sea. Whatever the reason, the Gribble had been munching to their hearts' content.

I looked at the other big jobs. The rib tops where she had been raised from an open boat and raised again in the seventies were actually a serious source of water ingress through the deck. This had been dealt with by the liberal application of a rubbery bitumen roofing sealer gloop. Where it had stuck, it worked; where it sat on top of the deck, it held the water underneath and just helped the rot on its way, silently, unseen until another drip fell on you in your bunk. Well, not my bunk, I am the skipper after all.

Well, that completed the work list: stop the leaks from above and below, remove any rotten timber, strengthen where necessary, completely replace as required. It became obvious that there would be little point in just doing the emergency work and ignoring the rest. It all had to be done or it wouldn't be a proper job. It was more a case of where to start rather than what to do. It seemed logical to start with the worst area, which had necessitated *Caronia* being lifted out in the first place. The offending sprung plank was cut out, cautiously at first, just removing the actual damaged area and no more. There was a lot of timber in this area and it seemed feasible to just make up a short repair plank and let it into the missing void.

It was some considerable time before this plank was replaced and it became the one-pound comment, as in, if I had received a pound for every time a passer-by commented, 'There's a hole in your boat,' I could have paid for the entire refit and sailed round the world.

Where the concrete had been poured in, it had sat and allowed rot to take hold of the first frame, particularly on the starboard side. A hammer chisel was used to chip away at the years-old panic repair and after a few hours a small heap of rubble lay under her bow as it showered from the now fully exposed missing plank.

The starboard side bad planks cut out, with a short template made as a guide for the new plank to come. Unfortunately the black holes were to grin at passers-by for many months to come.

The seriously decayed frame was cut out, bit by bit; these were early days and I was all too aware that if I simply removed everything that was suspect or showed signs of decay, I could very easily end up building a boat, not repairing one.

As it turned out, I need not have been too concerned. Although there is nothing more sad than a wooden boat with a missing plank or two, no matter how large the vessel the black hole draws your attention, like encountering a one-eyed pirate without his eye patch – an unpleasant image. In fact the vast majority of *Caronia*'s original hull was as sound and as strong as the day it was first fastened on the beach in Newlyn. Over the years her grown oak frames had taken on the resilience of iron as they had aged and hardened.

We decided to investigate the full extent of the areas to be replaced. There were the four bow planks, a sizeable section on the upper port bow, where she had been raised with inferior planking, a smaller section on the port quarter, a very rotten rudder post and the not insignificant problem of the short seventies rib tops that resembled a boxer's grin, out of line, a couple missing and nearly all loose. The options were to replace them one by one and realign them or the somewhat drastic step of cutting them all off at deck level, which is what we did. It was, in the end, the most logical thing to do. It allowed us to address one of the other considerable issues, which was the part-rotten and leaking deck. As with every other project on *Caronia*, all options were considered and then usually the most difficult and time-consuming undertaken.

The deck was a mixture of short and long planks with various repairs over the years, hence the rubber coating. I am sure we weren't the first to ponder the best way forward to try and achieve a watertight deck. After some research and talking with other owners and restorers, there seemed only one thing to do: basically clad the deck, but this time with a marine plywood skin and a top coat of epoxy matting. I was to regret the use of epoxy for many years to come. Not because it didn't do the job, but because I had a horrendous allergic reaction to it. Even now I can't even get a whiff of its pungent smell without my eyes prickling and itching.

There was no other option other than to cut the bad capping rail and rib tops off.

The very effective but horrendous epoxy sheathing on the foredeck.

Obviously it would have been ideal if we could have stripped the deck planks off and re-laid and caulked as we went. The trouble is, as with everything on boats, the deck plank is connected to the deck frame, which is connected to the beam shelf, which is connected to the ribs, which form the hull down to the keel; in short, start that kind of strip-down and you really will be left standing in a boatyard with nothing but a keel sitting on some blocks and a massive heap of firewood with no way back. I've seen a number of rebuilds go this way; clad and seal it had to be.

It was a nerve-wracking day when I took a saw to the old rib tops, working one by one with a handsaw, and the tops and capping rail, which was in fact old flooring, along with the small bulwark plank were cut loose and dropped to the ground. This allowed the decayed toe plank on the port and starboard bow, along with other bad areas, to be removed. We stood back and looked at the weekend's work. Holes, missing planks, no rib tops, no bulwarks and no capping rail. As with all rebuilds, whether old buildings, vehicles, or boats, you have to get rid

Just some of the cutting out that had to be done on the 1930s work.

of the bad to be able to start rebuilding with good. It still looked pretty daunting though and I was almost embarrassed at the heap of detritus that now lay on the ground.

It looked like we had a fair bit to do, and just to finish things off the small mizzen mast was lowered and the rubber deck coating ground off. We tried every way possible to remove this material – chisels, heat gun, and electric plane. Where it had stuck it did not want to let go, which was pretty much all over the deck except for bad patches on the starboard quarter, port amidships and port bow. We used flap-wheel angle grinders and it really was a filthy nightmare of a job, which sent up so much smoke that the marina office manager actually came over thinking we were ablaze. After the stripping, grinding, cutting and dumping of rotten wood we reached a point where there was no more going backwards and it was time to start sourcing, shaping and fitting some new timber.

The pitch pine that makes up the original planking of *Caronia* is no longer easily available. The trees that grew to form her hull were long ago felled and supply is exhausted. It is possible to get imported kiln-dried pitch pine but the drying destroys the very thing about pitch pine that is its best asset: the high, almost wet sap content, which gives it the resistance to water and rot. Other options were looked at such as hardwoods or other, readily available, types of resilient softwood. It would have been prohibitively expensive to use hardwood for all the repairs necessary so it had to be softwood. I am not sure how I hit upon the idea but I think it was while working on a building project and talking to the carpenter who was laying some outside patio decking. Pressure-treated decking. Brainwave: make all the woodwork and have it pressure treated, in effect a modern, albeit chemical, pitch pine.

Over the next few weeks all the bad decking timber and the port and starboard upper timber that had been cut out was replicated, treated and secured in place. There were a few of the 1933 raising ribs on the port side that also needed replacing. These were now under the deck level and had suffered from the incoming fresh water from the bad seventies rib tops above. One of the first photos I took of my son while working on the rebuild was of him using an electric plane to shape one of these ribs. The deck was skinned over in ply, which also allowed for the lower areas to be built up and the ply then epoxy coated.

The early picture of Lewis with an electric planer. No Play Stations here!

Ply covering the deck and building up the low areas by multiple laminating to give a fall off the deck.

The built-up port side where the water used to gather to an inch deep.

The partly clad foredeck, under which is the skipper's cabin and a now-dry bunk.

The completed foredeck.

The clad side decks.

New rib tops above deck level were cut, by eye. This meant each one was slightly different, as they would have been when first made by nothing but hand tools. They were pressure-treated, bonded to the epoxied deck and secret screwed down. The same process was utilised for the bulwarks and capping rails. Stand back, take stock. Not bad!

Cutting the new rib tops by eye but with the aid of modern power tools.

The new rib tops lined up in place, ready for fixing.

The new capping rail, again cut by eye, prior to pressure treating.

The capping rail, scarf jointed together.

The rib tops, now with the capping rail fixed in place.

The new bulwarks, capping rail and rubbing strake on the port side.

It didn't take long for the new timber to start going in and the badly rotted port side to start looking sound again.

Nearly there with the new ribs.

The port side fully repaired and sound once more.

Lewis with the new portside toe rail, the old one having rotted due to the bad rib tops.

The toe rail cut and shaped into place ready for fastening.

The port side, now clad in marine ply and epoxy to keep out the dreaded fresh water.

It was during the last stages of getting the rib tops and rails on that I started to look at and plan the work on the hull. I had decided to get *Caronia* surveyed by a wooden boat specialist. I would need a full survey for insurance when the work was complete so it seemed a good idea to have one done at this stage so we had a 'to do' list to work to that would satisfy an insurer. It would also be useful to have another pair of eyes look over her should the survey find anything I hadn't yet seen or missed altogether. Ted the surveyor, a man with a reputation for dealing with wooden boats, arrived and cast an eye over *Caronia*'s hull. The black holes grinned at him and I am sure he didn't mean to, but he couldn't help saying, 'There's holes in your boat.' That's two pounds, as it was the plural. Ted retired not long after he dealt with *Caronia*, but I don't think the two events were connected.

It took him most of the day to crawl in, over, under and around *Caronia*'s hull and decks. I think it was only the repaired deck that gave him faith that we would and could tackle the extra list of repairs that would be required before *Caronia* could be lifted back into the water. Most of the items on his list I already knew about but seeing it in black and white made me realise just how much there was still to do.

3

Real Progress

Sometimes things just fall into place. I had started thinking that to move things forward I may have to get some help with *Caronia*. My business was doing well, which was a plus for finances but only left me with the weekends to work on her. Lewis was still at school and played rugby on Sundays, which only gave him Saturdays with me. So at that time progress was slow. I was talking to an old friend in the local one night and he told me of a shipwright he knew who had just been made redundant. I met Mark at *Caronia* and we discussed a list of jobs. Rather than us tackling everything between us, we split the work, with him using his many years of experience to take on the hull work, and me concentrating on the internal frames that needed replacing. In the end we both worked on the hull, nailing, fastening and caulking. 40 feet of boat, 80 feet of seams per plank, yard after yard of cotton caulking. It was a long job.

There were times when just having Mark as a sounding board made all the difference. *Caronia* had been out of the water for far longer than I had ever intended and had dried and her seams had opened up. I saw this as a bad thing but to Mark it allowed loose planks to be found, old caulking dragged out and fresh seams hammed in. I found caulking to be one of the most satisfying jobs. Gently tapping in the very thing that would keep the sea out and allow *Caronia*'s old hull to float once more.

When it came to the four bad planks on her bow, having someone with the experience of Mark, and in no small way his contacts, was again a blessing. We cut the four planks back several feet to cross a number of ribs, including the new bow one I had made from a single piece of iroko. We borrowed an old Frankenstein steamer box and boiler from Mark's old yard. We repaired it with new copper tube, made new planks out of green larch and quite simply steamed, jacked, dragged and hammered the new planks into place. They were faired in, sanded, caulked and primer painted.

It was the first time in many months I really felt that *Caronia* would return to the sea after all. Mark had now been with me for about six weeks – not long considering how long *Caronia* was out of the water in total, but the amount we achieved in that time was significant. Sometimes, no matter how strong your spirit, everyone needs a little help.

Some of the yards and yards of caulking cotton that went in to making her watertight again.

Mark the shipwright in his usual pose, on his knees tapping in caulking.

A new frame made in two halves to replace the rotted out bow frame.

The new bow frame in place with its other half, repairing damage done many years ago.

That missing plank again, but now with a new one made and ready to go in.

Lewis learning another new skill: soldering up a new steam pipe for the steamer box.

The steamer box at work.

Three hours of hot steam and the planks were ready to work.

The first new plank going in and those holes finally being filled.

Clamps used to hold the front of the new plank.

Props on the port side to hold the new planks in place.

Driving in yet more of those square ship nails known as dumps.

Done – no more passers by pointing to the missing planks.

Fairing in the new planks.

Finally painted and looking like they had been there for years.

Fourteen of the first futtocks, the main frames or ribs which lay across the keel, had split as a result of her keel moving. It would have meant destroying most of her belly to take them out so the recognised method is to sister such damaged frames. In other words, make a new frame to sit alongside the damaged one and bolt the two together. Each frame was made from 10 x 3 inch, 6-foot-long iroko beams. I didn't use hardwood for any particular reason. I could, as I later did with the engine bearers, have used oak railway sleepers; the iroko was cheap and, being a hardwood, very stable and less likely to move or warp once fitted.

The new frames were shaped and, with *Caronia*'s almost flat bottom, only required a small taper to be taken from the end of each beam. They were then bolted in, through the existing first and second futtocks and right down through the oak keel, keel ballast and steel keel shoe, with very large galvanised studding. Drilling holes over 2 feet with a 22 mm diameter drill is no small task and I could be found literally sitting on a massive slow-speed electric drill for hours at a time before giving a cheer as daylight and the ground could be seen through another completed hole!

The new keel frames or first futtocks.

One of the bits of large galvanised studding used to secure the new frames to the keel.

That big drill, through the frame, keel and keel shoe.

Another one done after pushing the drill for hours.

The new frames in place and another much needed repair completed.

Spurred on by the now sound hull, the repaired and strengthened frames and the watertight deck, I looked at the next area needing attention. The survey had shown up a problem with the rudder post, a 5-inch-square lump of timber that is attached to the aft of the keel and runs up the inside of the transom. It looked OK from the outside but in fact this was only due to the layers of paint covering the horror below. Even a gentle poke with a knife blade revealed that under the paint very little wood existed. No problem. After the deck, ribs, frames and planks, this was by comparison a small, self-contained job. If working with 5-inch-square, 5-foot-long lengths of hardwood can ever be described as a small job.

There was one slight issue with replacing the rudder post; the rudder had to come off. I don't know what *Caronia*'s steel rudder weighs – enough to require some form of mechanical handling, as in a block and tackle. Once off, I could just about move it around;

Removing the old rudder post. It didn't take much cutting out as it was so rotten.

Not a day for working on boats. The rudder is seen laying off in the snow.

I would think it's in excess of 250 pounds. As well as the rudder, the stocks or hinges had to be removed, which was fortunate as it revealed that the bronze bolts holding the stocks to the post were seriously corroded and didn't really unscrew so much as snap and fall off. I didn't even begin to picture the now avoided moment when the twelve rotted bolts gave way, letting the 250 pound rudder sink to the bottom of the sea, mid-Channel, with a storm coming and the tide just turning against us; I thought it best to stop thinking about it at that point.

There wasn't much woodwork required in making the new post; it was, after all, a big square lump of timber. I had a piece of iroko the right size in my heap of useful bits of wood and it was drilled and bolted in place. The knee that forms a right-angle brace between the keel and the post was as good as the day it had first been made, so it was returned to its original location along with the rudderstocks, which went back on with new bolts. For such an important repair it actually only took a couple of days and gave me a real boost in moral. Instead of the never-ending, or so it seemed, sanding, caulking and nailing, having worked our way through a big sack of hundreds of big square 'dumps' or square ship nails, to do a job that was completed so quickly was a real sense of achievement.

The day I lifted the rudder back on, I actually stood back and thought to myself that, if I wanted to, we could relaunch what was now a sound and watertight boat with a working engine and once she had taken up, swollen to squeeze the caulking, then the sound of incoming water would be just a memory and something to write about.

The original knee bolted back in.

The new rudder post secured
to the old knee and transom.

The truth was we still needed to paint and antifoul, but as we had sanded and all new timber had been primed, we could have relaunched sporting a colour scheme that wouldn't have looked out of place as she sailed to war, a dark, if not battleship grey.

Of course, in reality there was still plenty to do before *Caronia* could go back in the doubled-up slings required to spread her weight in the travel lift and be lowered back into her natural element. All the deck furniture had been removed in the first week to allow the deck repair. By deck furniture I mean the mast tabernacles, fairleads, ventilators, deck lights and, by no means least, the massive oversize bronze mooring bollards. These are some 21 by 8-inch slabs with two paint-tin-size horns made entirely of solid bronze. I, after an extra Weetabix, had manged to rope them to the ground but now utilised a Bailey bridge construction to chain-winch them back on deck. This took the form of an aluminium ladder ratchet strapped through the two doors of the wheelhouse, but it worked and the bollards were bolted back slightly aft of their original positions to allow them a better alignment with the bulwark fairleads I had built from scratch out of some huge salvaged hardwood doors. The deck-mounted fairleads were now shunned as I didn't want anything screwed through the new sealed deck if I could avoid it.

The hardwood fairleads have now been in use for over seven years and are just about showing the merest rope rubbing in the corner – not bad for something the doubters said would wear right through in weeks. They are much like her original oak frames and just seem to get tougher with age.

The massive, almost solid bronze mooring bollards.

A bit of a rig but the only way to get the overweight bollards back on board.

The little signature left by her mooring ropes add character to her and remind me of the now covered thumb-deep rope rubs in her toe rails that had been slowly etched into her by her bindings and the wash of passing vessels heading out to sea during her long confinement in Shoreham Harbour.

4

The End of the Beginning

I took another look at what was left to do and realised that apart from the painting there were two jobs that would require some thought and not inconsiderable effort. Four or so years previously, when the Leyland engine had been installed, we had dropped in the 1500 BMC wing engine. It was on temporary engine beds and there was no propeller shaft or shaft tunnel. Inside the engine room there was an old lead sheet plate attached to a hull frame just behind the BMC. I don't know when the wing engine had been removed; I would think it may have been when she returned to fishing and the rumoured Gardener engine had been installed.

When the lead bung was removed, it revealed a hole through the frame to a patched outer hull. A long drill bit was used to follow the line of the frame hole and out through the hull. A lager hole saw cut back from outside and a boat jumble bargain stern tube, shaft and propeller was slid in through the access hole. As I slid it in, it fouled on something and several attempts failed to get it any further. I called up to Lewis through the hole to see what it was getting hung up on. He shouted back that I better come and take a look.

The wing engine propeller being offered into place.

The wing shaft up
against the gearbox
of the 1500 BMC.

So for the umpteen thousandth time I climbed up the ladder, expecting to find yet another problem in the endless long list of problems.

I could really do without this, I thought. I really did want to relaunch as soon as possible and had even contemplated not doing the wing engine work on this lift out.

Lewis pointed to the 'problem': there was the end of the shaft I had been trying to slide into place and it was indeed hitting something. It was hitting smack bang dead-centre into the gearbox shaft coupling of the BMC. In other words, the wing engine on its temporary beds was spot on in the right position.

I suppose sometimes some things can just work like that but it was a very welcome shortcut after so many months of hard work. The temporary beds had still been made to securely carry the weight of the BMC and were entirely fit for the purpose of carrying the engine under any power. All that was needed was some fairing or angled pieces of timber to be cut to sit at the front of the BMC to match up the the incoming propeller tube and shaft angle.

The long length of stern tube outside the hull required a pod or nacelle to carry it and secure it to the hull. The woodwork was shaped from some greenheart timber, the kind used on breakwaters and beach defences. It was made in two halves to allow the centre to be gouged out to accommodate the stern tube. Timber was also shaped and fitted inside the hull to carry the stern gland and house the shaft. Everything was bolted together and through the hull. I drilled a large hole in the top of the inner timber to allow for the pouring in of some kind of sealant to bond the tube and inner and outer timbers to the hull. Traditionally, old left-over lead-based paint was used for this, or pitch or anything else that would form a semi-flexible seal around what is after all a very big hole through the hull.

I used a modern version of pitch; it's more a rubberised compound, probably in the same family as the dreadful stuff we had ground off the deck months before. It was melted in a boiling pot and poured in the access hole to fill the void. All I can say is it worked, and on launching it was one of the few areas that didn't let water in.

Part of the shaft nacelle with the gouge taken out for the stern tube.

The nacelle bolted together and ready to go on.

Final offering up to make sure it all fits.

Wing engine nacelle bolted to the hull and ready for the stern tube.

It was a few more months until the BMC was finally linked up with the new shaft and put to the test for the first time. It does propel us along very well, albeit very slowly, and the steering is poor as the propeller is off to the port side, but if the intention is to at least keep on going in the direction you want and to be able to keep her head into the wind and waves, then the little BMC does the job well. I was going to add to this paragraph that now we have installed the brand-new Perkins, the BMC may never be needed, but as any seafarer will know, standing on deck saying, 'Well it's not as rough as I thought it was going to be,' is asking for trouble and usually followed by the biggest, blackest cloud you've ever seen rolling over you and the immediate splash of cold water straight in your face. I will simply say that it is a very comforting feeling to know that down in the engine room there are two power plants, two propeller shafts, two fuel systems and two bronze screws out the back.

Another stand and look session. *Caronia* had been out of the water for so long now I didn't want to get her back in and to go ahead with the launch while all the time something else was bothering me. It was obvious that the painting still need to be finished. The first coat of bright blue was looking striking; it shone in the sunlight and really gave the big hull some presence. I had given a lot of thought to the final colour scheme; it is best to paint wooden boats as light a colour as possible to resist warming by the sun and expansion and contraction damage. *Caronia* had over the years been a rainbow of colour schemes and during the refit we had sanded through the best part of fifteen coats in some places. I am sure I went through some battleship grey from her navy days and right down, right close to the wood, I found blue.

In my mind that had to be her oldest colour and on many visits around Cornish harbours a wide range of bright paints could be seen, but blue tended to be the prominent scheme used. Cornish blue is a fairly pale, almost washed-out finish, so blue with the benefit of a light colour to resist sun damage, but I had seen several boats with bright in-your-face blue, almost the startling colours found on the Greek island fishing boats. So bright, shiny, vibrant blue it was to be. She still is in her bright colour and it makes her stand out at events and festivals, or as a film star.

The first time the new bright blue paint saw the sunshine.

The red boot top line, which was to peel off on the way to London.

The only difference now is we use a good old-fashioned oil-based household paint. It has far more body than marine enamel and after her last makeover following the rigors of filming in May 2016 we lifted her out and within three weeks had completed a total repaint. When lifted back in, the Dulux Weather Shield had sufficient flex not to crack along the caulking lines as the hull compressed under her own weight.

Back in 2010 the real problem when trying to paint was the weather; it was, politely put, very unkind to us. The marine-grade paints we used back then take an extremely long time to dry, anything up to ten hours on cooler days. If they aren't dry when it starts to damp down in the evening then the paint dulls and takes on a milky hue and has to be rubbed back for another coat to be applied.

An unusual picture: an old Cornish fishing boat at the modern Canary Wharf.

This happened again and again. Lewis and I used to drive to the yard from home and scrutinise the dashboard thermometer. Years later, the chorus of 'too cold to paint' still sang out as we drove to building sites when Lewis apprenticed to me.

The result of this coat on coat was that a couple of years later, as we steamed to the Diamond Jubilee Pageant, the blue paint peeled from our sides like some kind of nautical Russian doll until in places we were back to the grey primer. Maybe *Caronia* was trying to relive her war time colour scheme. When we arrived in Canary Warf I had to lean over the side with a brush tied to a boat hook and patch her up as best as possible. On the day we sailed in that proud convoy down the Thames, the weather was so bad and the rain so heavy I don't think anyone would have noticed if *Caronia* had been blue, grey or pink! With the painting finally done there was no ignoring it – one last massive job before relaunch. *Caronia*'s keel had a significant 'hog', a bend or curve upwards. This mattered not when she sat in the forgiving medium of water but she had been built to take the ground, meaning she could come ashore and sit on her keel and beaching whales, the double-thickness hull on her round bilges: exactly what she would have done many times in the drying harbour of St Ives.

Now the keel was curved upwards by years of gentle aging and movement of the timber. Some old wooden boat boys said it was because she had been designed to carry many tons of fish in her hold and without this constant weight, her amidships had lifted by the release of the tension built in to take the bulk of the fish.

It is possible the hog had grown into her over the years and her carvel planking had slowly moved alongside its neighbouring plank until the curve settled. It's just as possible that she was actually built like that as her keel sat on the sea-curved surface of that Cornish beach. Whatever the cause, the middle of the keel was now nearly 4 inches out of line and if we sat on the sand her increased bulk and ballast would break her own back.

With the new iroko frames inside and the massive bolts pulling her all together again, the keel was sound and strong, just bent. There was no way any amount of dragging and clamping with new timber inside would have ever pulled her flat again; the hog had formed over eight plus decades, or been built there. The only solution would be to sister the keel underneath and shape the top of the sister keel to fit into the curve of the hog but maintain a totally flat lower edge.

That sounds easy enough. I would need some 10 inch by 6 inch timber, preferably hardwood, and I would need about 40 feet of it. As with the timber search for the later new masts, it didn't take too much research to find out that hardware shops and most timber yards don't keep that kind of woodwork. I rang a local saw mill. 'Hi, I need 10 inch by 6 inch by 40 feet of oak.' The answer was yes, no problem, that's the kind of thing they did as they supplied the timber-frame building trade and at that time bespoke large frame oak timber buildings were very much in fashion. 'That will be £1,450.00 plus VAT. Plus cutting, handling and transport.' I thought for a moment, then asked a couple more questions: in two bits, in three, in four?

It still came close to the original price no matter which way they cut it. It occurred to me I may never get this opportunity again so I went for it. 'You do know this stuff grows on trees don't you?' There was a silence then the phone went dead. I suppose a sense of humour is a personal thing. Oh, well – I would have to think of something else.

The large timber-frame buildings had got me thinking of who else uses such bulky woodwork. Architectural garden designers use all kinds of large timber, especially railway sleepers. There was the answer – railway sleepers. Relatively cheap and easy to come by. I wouldn't need top-quality ones; after all, they were going to be bolted to the underside of a boat and covered in antifoul. A quick search on the now ever-growing e-Bay and I had found no end of reclamation yards selling old sleepers. Except they were all 8 inches by 6 inches and covered in bitumen and tar. Re-enter search to 'new' railway sleepers and there they were; 10 inches by 6, 10 feet long. £30 each and brand new, untreated. I am not too bad with mental arithmetic so it didn't take too long to work out that even driving to Bristol in my big pickup truck, the sleepers were a bargain. By the weekend I had collected them and literally dropped them off the truck at the work heap alongside *Caronia*.

The next process may sound a little bit easier than it actually was. Shape the tops of the sleepers and bolt them on. Job done. To achieve this, the shores or large wooden blocks that *Caronia* sat on had to be moved to allow access to at least 10 feet of her keel at a time to get the sister keel up under her. I work on the principle that if I am going to take one block out, I put two in beforehand. You really can't take chances under a 40-ton boat; years of working on lorries and cars with my dad had taught me that.

Making use of some leverage to shift the bulky oak railway sleepers.

After shifting the blocks, I wriggled the four new lump of timber into place with rollers and utilised levers to shift their bulk. The guy in the yard I had got them from told me they weighed 110 kg each, that's 242 pounds or over 17 stone. Just a bit lighter than me actually, and slightly less stubborn to shift. It would have been less of a struggle had Lewis, who is built like the proverbial Thames tugboat, a strong addition to the workforce and keen ruby player, not been sitting on the sidelines taking pictures as I struggled with the bulk of the keel timbers while he displayed a homage to his rugby club in the form of a purple, green and white plaster cast on his match-broken ankle.

In deference to his spirit he did still manage to drag himself under *Caronia* to paint on coat after coat of base primer on her hull. I think it was the first modern paint she had ever seen below the waterline as we had sanded, ground and scraped off a paint and bitumen antifoul mixture. He would return to his mum with the tricolour cast now sporting silver-grey highlights. Character building stuff. Made him the man he is today and definitely not a form of workhouse child cruelty.

I could have used some long off-cuts of plywood to make a template and save having to shift the sleepers more than once but I didn't have anything suitable and I wanted to see how they actually looked under the hull. The old 'if it looks right, it is' thing. Having got them in place, I marked them across from the curved keel onto the sleeper and used a high-tech string line to ensure a flat underside.

Not traditional but an electric chainsaw is faster than an adz.

The sister keels in place and awaiting bolting on.

Thank goodness for power tools. An adze or spoke shave would have been more traditional but an electric chainsaw and tungsten-bladed electric planer made short work of the cutting and shaping. A liberal coat of a roofing sealer bitumen gloop was applied to the top and the sister keels were hydraulically jacked up under *Caronia*'s original keel.

I had thought about extending the long galvanised bolts that had been used to secure the iroko sister frames to the keel, but decided that as that was a completed job and the sister keel was in effect a ballast keel, I would bolt it on with fish plates and not disturb the completed work. Apart from a reasonable amount of pushing and shoving, the sisters went on well and gave *Caronia* a very strong and solid battering ram of a keel. It reminded me of pictures I had seen of warships with strengthened keels designed for running down submarines. It would certainly be an interesting encounter if one of the 'power gives way to sail' risk-takers ever cut too close to our path and expected me to stop *Caronia* on a sixpence.

On the day of the relaunch the sister keels can be seen bolted on and filling the hog in the old keel.

The new keel had been tapered so that she will sit with the deck pretty much level if we take the ground. When I collected the new sleepers I mentioned to the yardman that they were an unusual size; he said they were a standard size used in France. I haven't told *Caronia* her keel is French.

Rolling in a beam sea had been a bit of a problem with *Caronia*; all boats roll in a beam or side-on sea but *Caronia* had the ability to dip her high gunnels into the wavetops. You always felt safe and like she could take it, scared but safe. In truth, if I had known about the split frames and honeycomb planks I might not have been so confident. Previously an owner had fitted bilge keels, extra short keels along the bilge curves of the hull. These had long ago rotted or fallen off. I had considered bilge keels and they would have helped to prevent some of her rolling but with her tonnage they couldn't have supported her on the sand and may well have just torn off. Maybe this is what had happened to the previous ones.

The new deeper keel and low weight were bound to help stabilise her and it was nice to know there was that amount of solid wood under us as we bumped on the beach while re-enacting *Caronia*'s finest hour on the beaches of Dunkirk during the filming of the Warner Brother epic *Dunkirk*.

In fact *Caronia* still rolled 'like a drunken kitten in wet grass', as one passenger remarked as they slowly turned the colour of said grass. But now at least, with all the extra woodwork and bolts, we could enjoy the experience of watching the waves wash her decks while clinging on for dear life in the wheelhouse!

5

Relaunch

One of the final jobs before relaunching was putting the ballast back in; tons and tons of pig iron, rough-cast lumps of cast iron that had been taken out at the start of the refit to allow access to the inside of the hull. I had weighed some of it on some old bathroom scales I had found in a bin; a count up, a few calculations: 9 tons – 9 tons of pig iron, loads of flattened lead pipe and 200 block pavers, which we had added some years previously in an effort to steady her. I looked at all the extra timber that had been installed and the sheer weight of it and decided to dump over half the pavers in the builder's skip that someone had conveniently put close by. Since then the rest have been ditched as well.

We painted the pig iron with bitumen to help prevent corrosion – a long, laborious and messy task and something we were to curse for years to come as the bitumen managed to find its way onto everything. Boots, hands, ladders, tea cups, sandwiches, and on one occasion, while spending a night sleeping on an old mattress inside the stripped-out hull, I awoke to find I had rolled into a patch of bitumen and my face was stuck to the hull.

The pig iron was loaded on pallets and before the boat yard went too health and safety I used the forklift to raise them up to deck level and a chain gang of my staff loaded them below decks. Iron ballast in wooden boats is one of those dark subjects. Ideally you don't want the iron touching or sitting on the inside of the hull, but in reality there really isn't anywhere else to put it other than to fill the spaces between the lower frames. Some boats have bespoke castings that hook over the frame and keep the metal off the hull. No such luxury with *Caronia*, with every bit of space needing to be filled to give her the ballast required for her bulbous hull to sit to her waterline. The way she sits almost planted in the water prompted one visiting surveyor to remark, 'She's as stiff as a church,' as he walked around her decks.

Then, one sunny day after the twelve-week proposed refit had slightly over-run to ninety-three weeks (I prefer 'just under two years' – it somehow doesn't sound so long but in truth gives little indication of the ninety-three weekends, not every one but most of them spent in, on or under *Caronia*), she was lifted back into the slings of the travel lift. I sent Lewis a mobile phone picture at school as her keel touched the water after so long: 'Ninety-three weeks and she's in!!'

Back in the travel lift after occupying that corner of the yard for many months.

Caronia was to hang in the slings overnight to allow time for take up, for her planks and caulking to swell, without the risk of joining so many of her wartime companions on the bottom of the sea. The disconcerting sound of incoming water that had prompted her lift-out so long before could unfortunately be heard everywhere. I mean, there were dry bits but on the whole the hull was leaking, badly.

I think I hit a low point right then. After so many months of work it felt like we had achieved nothing. The reason for the lift-out was to cure leaks not create more. Logic had to take over: her planks had dried and shrunk, the caulking cotton was bone-dry and it was only really the putty that was sealing what had become in some places very open seams. Just wait, I told myself, keep the pumps going, keep an eye on her, keep pumping.

In the end I decided to go and get a bag of chips and stop fussing; she was in the slings and going nowhere. I returned two hours later, chips and tea consumed, and found that well over 80 per cent of the incoming water had stopped. That's the advantage of cotton caulking – it takes up very quickly. I dealt with the worst seams by brass nailing small battens over them with some sealer underneath. That worked and bit by bit the hum of the automatic bilge pump grew less and less. I decided to go home to bed, get a good night's sleep and come back in the morning.

As the sun came up I was standing on the jetty next to *Caronia*; she looked happy sitting with the water just on her boot top line and although still supported like some drunk by the

Her keel is wet for the first time in nearly two years.

four webbing straps, she was indeed afloat. I felt we should have played some bagpipes or blessed her in some way. I just thought it was a blessing to have relaunched.

A bit later that morning a couple of the guys who worked for me came down to the yard and we, under her own power, took her across to her new mooring in Chichester Marina. We had let our old mooring in Birdham Pool go: simple as we hadn't been there for so long. *Caronia* had the last laugh: as we neared our pontoon and while pulling on a rope, one of the lads, Simon, stepped backwards straight into the water. Well, we all thought it was amusing but not quite the splash of champagne on the bow stem that is customary.

Less than nine days later Lewis and I set off to go to the 2010 Dunkirk Return, the five-yearly gathering of surviving Dunkirk Little Ships and the crossing back to the beaches of Dunkirk. It would have been Lewis's first voyage to Dunkirk and a very significant journey to make after so much work.

The story of that voyage is worth telling in its own right. It was emotional for many reasons and even though we didn't make it to Dunkirk, it meant so much. Mechanical problems and bad weather held us first in Eastbourne for five days and then in Dover for a further seven. The mechanical problems were within our power to repair but there was nothing we could do about the easterly wind which brought the sea crashing into the outer harbour wall off Dover.

Above: Stuck in the Granville Lock at Dover, 2010. Nothing to look at but the wall.

Left: In Ramsgate harbour having met up with the rest of the Dunkirk fleet.

We did have one go at getting out but it was so bad we had to scurry straight back in. After so long out the water, *Caronia* was going to take months, not the days it had been since the relaunch, for her planks to swell again and to get her strength back. At that time she was more akin to a Venetian blind of slats that could move independently of each other. We just dared not push her too hard.

We had to seek permission to return straight back into Dover by the commercial eastern entrance having exited via the small craft western as we just couldn't turn round in the unpleasant swell, which was sending waves breaking over the bow and ship's dog Wilson as he performed some kind of re-enactment of the storm scene in *Forrest Gump*. I am sure he actually barked, 'Is this all you've got?' before we dragged him back into the wheelhouse for safety and he took on the alias of Lieutenant Dog.

We did get up to Ramsgate on the one fine day in ages and the same day the Small Ship fleet got back across from Dunkirk. To us it was a triumph and proved we could do it and had done it after all the months of work.

6

New Power

Since the major refit, the work and adventures have continued. We got out on *Caronia* whenever we could and rebuilt some of the interior in a completely different style to how she had been prior to everything being removed for access. There was still the issue of the old Leyland engine; before this was resolved, it was difficult to plan and install the final interior fit-out. We attended the Diamond Jubilee Pageant in 2012, again another adventure worthy of its own book and another great adventure for all the family crew, which now included Natalie's partner Adam. With respect to the old Leyland, it was a fitting end to her service as a marine engine and a kind of swansong.

I approached Perkins in the hope that they might fancy sponsoring an old Dunkirk Little Ship with a new engine. I sent pictures of us sailing down the Thames, just passing the Houses of Parliament. I sent them her history and a list of all the things we had done on her and with her. I wrote a letter claiming, 'There is no way this piece of British maritime heritage should ever be fitted with an engine that was made east of the white cliffs of Dover or west of the Lizard.'

The *Caronia* family: Me, Natalie, Lewis and ship's dog Wilson. The H24 is our fleet number for the pageant.

Another great picture. *Caronia* in the Thames, just passing Big Ben.

I thought it was a great pitch and worthy of *Dragons' Den*, but the short answer was no. In fairness, and with great thanks to Perkins, they did do me a fantastic deal and I don't see how it can have been much more than the build cost to them. It suited me better and meant it was now my engine and not a freebie.

The subject of the new power plant had been a topic of considerable discussion – OK, argument – between Lewis and me. Having spent many long oily and diesel-soaked hours in the engine room nursing the poor old Leyland and with a mind to the future without the ever-present smell of both those engine fluids on your bedding, clothing, hair, skin and everywhere else, I remember actually laughing out loud when Christmas shopping, having spotted the perfume counter in Army and Navy advertising Diesel for Men, I remarked to the assistant, 'I've been wearing that for years.'

I really did lean towards a commercial quality but modern-build new power plant. Lewis was in favour of a classic engine such as the low revving Gardner much favoured by fishermen. There is no doubt that had we bought *Caronia* with the Gardner she is listed as once having, I would have done all I could to have rebuilt it and kept it. The problem was getting a Gardner at reasonable cost to rebuild and the not insurmountable cost of spares, or get an already rebuilt unit with the considerable cost of that option. With the country-wide availability of spares, the Perkins had to be the obvious choice and the deal from them made it a one-horse race.

Arrangements were made for delivery of the new engine and, after making the necessary booking with the yard, I put the old Leyland on that well-known internet auction site to raise some funds. In 2013 *Caronia* was again lifted out under the big travel lift at Chichester and we repeated the roof-off process, although this time the new wheelhouse had been designed to allow this to be done without the aid of a power saw.

The Perkins 'Bertram' in the engine room. We couldn't get many pictures of the engine swap as the difficult situation with the yard meant we just had to get on with it.

We installed a brand-new, straight out the crate Perkins M130C, again six-cylinder and 6 litres but with all the reliability of a modern power plant.

It was a real flag day when the new engine dropped in except for the unpleasant interference of a building firm who were redeveloping the yard and stopped my engine lift crane coming in for several hours, and a site foreman whose use of the English language made even *Caronia* blush.

For better trim and to allow access down the aft ladder to what would become the crew quarters, the Perkins was to be installed a whole engine's length further forward. The new engine location of course required a longer prop shaft and the bigger power plant required a much larger propeller, taking us from the inadequate 19-inch three-bladed screw on the 3.4 BMC to a 22-inch three-blade on the Leyland and finally a massive 27-inch, four-blade bespoke work of sculpture on the Perkins.

In fact, when it arrived from the marine specialist I stood it in the corner of my kitchen just to look at in the couple of months before it was finally attached to the new and equally expensive and larger 2 inch diameter, much longer propeller shaft.

I wanted the new prop to sit further aft, away from the hull and in cleaner water, but the stern tube couldn't be removed – it just wouldn't budge. I guess the paint-bitumen combination, similar to Percy's prop shaft, had done a good job of sealing it in. I therefore got some bronze tubing and, not having a lathe that big, got it machined into an extension piece with a female thread to screw onto the existing shaft and a male thread to take the cutlass bearing carrier. Luckily both the stern gland and cutlass had inserts that I machined out on my lathe to accommodate the larger shaft.

I got the feeling I was reversing work done many years ago when *Caronia*'s large, powerful engine had been removed and the much smaller BMC 3.4 harbour engine had been installed, and a much lighter 1½-inch shaft had been fitted as opposed to the 2½-inch shaft the tube and glands could have carried.

By freehand sanding with a small angle grinder and flap wheel, I made a fairing-in piece, again out of some oak railway sleeper, to smooth in the very flat deadwood at the end of the keel and to better feed the sea onto the large propeller without cavitation (the effect when a propeller just can't get enough water). More sealant and large galvanised coach screws, the ones with a wood screw not the ones with nuts, were used to fix it in place. The cutlass housing went on with a new bearing, then the new propeller.

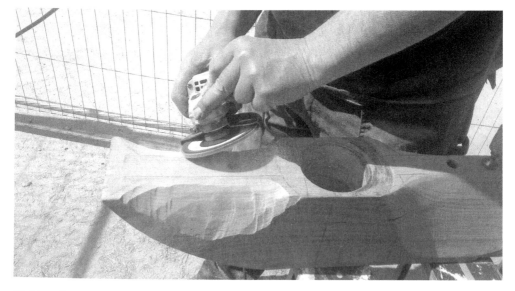

Making the fairing-in piece for the back of the keel deadwood.

Above left: The fairing-in piece in place to help prevent cavitation.

Above right: That monster of a new four-bladed bronze propeller. Seemed a shame to antifoul it.

Lewis and I looked at the new prop – it really was a piece of engineering art and it seemed a shame to paint it with the required protection and anti-foul. The front of the rudder was cut back with a leviathan of an angle grinder to give the required clearance behind the propeller and reduce interference.

The difference the new propeller has made to *Caronia* is staggering. The small prop that was fitted to the old 3.4 BMC reminded you of trying to whisk an omelette using your finger – you will get there but it took *Caronia* a long time to react to any input of drive. Peter the Leyland had a bigger prop and after engaging gear you at least felt like *Caronia* would get moving with some authority; the new four-blade work of bronze sculpture bites the sea the moment you push the gear lever into drive.

Even on tick-over we have immense control, and with the tendency for our left-handed propeller to walk to starboard when going astern, it makes coming along side on the starboard beam easy.

Grinding off some of the rudder to give clearance for the new propeller and prevent prop noise.

Due to a complicated set of physics, propellers want to 'walk', that is move sideways as opposed to just forward or aft when going ahead or astern. Simply thought of, a left-handed propeller will want to walk across the seabed to port when going ahead and to starboard when going astern. It's not actually interacting with the seabed but that's an easy way to understand the effect. The benefit is being able to come onto a pontoon at a slight angle and then not only arrest the forward motion of the boat but also skip her stern onto the mooring.

When coming in on a mooring to port it obviously has a very detrimental effect and pulls the stern away from the linesman who is kindly waiting to receive your ropes, sometimes taking the linesman with it. The knack is to know your boat and, in *Caronia's* 40-ton case, just come in slowly.

It wasn't the end of the line for Peter the Leyland engine either. The e-Bay advert had received absolutely no hits for days, then over the Saturday the page went mad; so did the phone. All the calls and enquires were from Welshmen – literally, all the calls. Curiosity got the better of me and upon enquiring I found out why. Nuffield tractors. All the interest was from the classic tractor world and the Leyland was the same as the ones fitted in the Nuffield. Only one call came from a local man, who came to look on behalf of a friend who wanted the engine for an 'Iron Fairy' crane, like one of those kids' Tonka toy square mobile cranes with the big wheels.

I was pleased the engine was going to continue a life in a classic vehicle. In truth I had only advertised it as I couldn't come to terms with the idea of just scrapping her after she had given us such faithful service.

By the time the engine had been lifted out and sold, the marine gearbox and engine mounts sold at Beaulieu Boat Jumble and, only just this year, the heat exchanger finally found a home, I was back to within £30 of what the Leyland had cost in the first place.

So that, to date, has brought us to the conclusion of the engine refits. The Perkins will last into the next generation of caretakers, most likely my daughter and son. We named the Perkins 'Bertram' after Admiral Bertram Ramsey, the commander of Operation Dynamo.

7

The Engine Room

Along with the new Perkins came the obvious desperate need to sort the fuel tanks and systems. The 3.4 had been fed by a 200-litre plastic tank, which was a repurposed water carrier. It had no baffles and seemed to have reacted with the diesel in it and bowed out at the sides. I had fitted a second, approximately 400-litre aluminium tank for longer range but its internal condition was unknown. It would constantly block filters and was a bit of a liability; with no inspection plate it couldn't be cleaned. We had for some time just run on the plastic tank. These issues and the problem that neither of them really fitted into the available space led to the logical conclusion that the only answer was new or even bespoke tanks.

There are marine manufactures who sell a range of off the shelf polypropylene tanks in various shapes, sizes and capacities, but not unsurprisingly none of them were the right shape or size for our needs. There was a useable space between Percy the BMC and the location where the new forward engine room bulkhead would be fitted. There was plenty of space on the starboard side as well.

An internet search found a firm not too far away and after making a timber frame mock up to confirm the measurements, an order was placed for two bespoke tanks. The day we went to collect, we were even shown around the factory to see how our order had been constructed.

Fitting the new tanks was a matter of again removing the upper aft section of the wheelhouse, as it had been designed to do. Stands were constructed and the tanks secured with strapping. They fit perfectly and the combined capacity of close on 600 litres is ample for our usual cruising range. The best thing is that with the aid of a torch you can actually see how much fuel there is in the tanks – no need to rely on inaccurate gauge systems.

A combined fuel filter and change over system completed the job and the new fuel installation. Either engine can draw from one or both tanks, and there are primer head filters with bypass to allow a filter to be changed and bled without having to shut an engine down. It seems strange even typing 'completed the job'; some of the projects on the boat have taken so long and seemed so never-ending that to start, work on, move forward and complete a job is sometimes hard to believe.

Above left: The port side tank in front of Percy.

Above right: The starboard side tank next to Bertram.

Although larger than the port tank, the starboard still had a sizeable space behind it within the confines of the engine room, the space on the port side being filled by Percy the BMC. It was an ideal space for a generator. So that's what we put there. The old, and hopefully to be refurbished, marine generator that had been dropped in at the same time as the Leyland originally went in was a no-go. It was just beyond repair.

I stripped it and removed it in bits. As with all the other leftovers off the boat, I took it to Beaulieu Boat Jumble and it sold – in bits, but it still sold. Despite the buyer asking if it worked, I looked into the box of dismembered machinery and the cracked cylinder head and assured him it should run fine but it may be out of warranty by the time he got home. *Caveat emptor.*

We don't have a lot of use for a generator as most of our trips and events are to locations where we can almost always pick up shore power. So I wanted the benefits of a generator without the very high cost of a water-cooled marine unit. The advantage of our engine room is the amount of space and ventilation, so an air-cooled unit would be suitable.

Right: The new fuel tanks going in, with the top section of the aft wheelhouse removed as it was designed to do.

Below: The fuel change over bank. Filters can be changed without shutting down an engine.

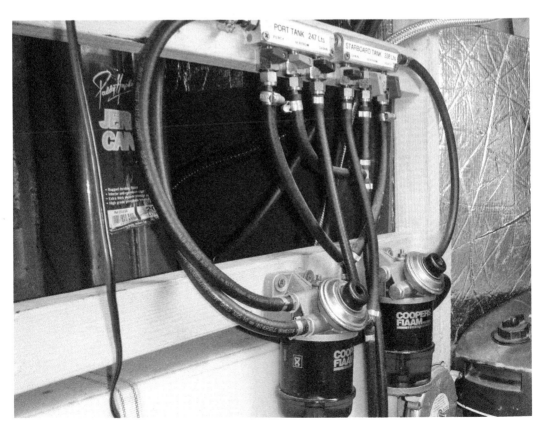

The cheapest generators are the kind used on building sites. A marine 3 kilowatt unit would have cost in excess of £3,000. For just under £300 I had a 3 kilowatt, 240/110 volt electric start framed generator delivered to my house.

Now here's the clever bit. As the most likely time for us to need an independent power source is when at one of our festivals but unable to get shore power (the kind of emergency when the batteries need charging or the beer fridge is getting warm), as we are usually rafted side by side and nobody likes a thumping, smelly diesel engine running, the generator is a quiet running petrol engine that I have converted to run on LPG from our two big storage cylinders under the wheelhouse seats.

Quiet, economical and virtually no smell of exhaust fumes. Green running, cold beer and even with the gas conversion, a tenth of the cost of a marine unit.

The gas-powered
3 kVA generator in the
engine room.

Bertram the big engine
in the now soundproofed
engine room.

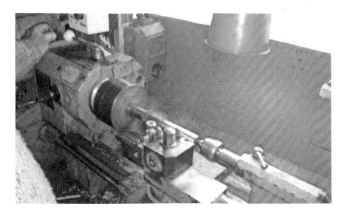

Above: Skimming the shaft of the steering head on my dad's lathe.

Right: Working on the steering head shaft.

We had reached a stage by now of having a sea-worthy vessel and actually considered revisiting some of the previously undertaken jobs. When the new Cornish wheelhouse had gone on, the old mechanical steering system had been stripped out in favour of a hydraulic system. It allowed the wheel to move further forward and clear a path to the port door. The hydraulics worked OK but were completely soulless. There was no feedback through the wheel and it just didn't suit *Caronia*. Lewis and I were keen to give *Caronia* back something from her past. The old chain steering had made a very familiar noise as the chains rattled through her hull to pull on the large tiller aft. So we decided to rebuild the steering head.

My dad still had a decent workshop with a lathe so we set up shop there. The cast iron leg of the steering head carried a shaft, which carried a cam, which engages into a male cog, which engages into a female cog, which turns a chain gypsy. It's as complex to watch it work as it is to describe. But it's a work of engineering genius and gives mechanical power steering onto the 3/8 chain.

An adjustable reamer was used to bit by bit take the wear out of the bearing journals until they were round again. The shaft was machined round and sleeved to suit the new journal size and a missing leg of the guide bar which acts as a locking mechanism was repaired.

When we refitted the head to *Caronia* it was moved forward to sit under the helm instruments and give a clear path to the port door like the hydraulic steering had, and also protect the rather aggressive in-running gears, which were not ideal for sticking a hand into in a rolling sea. New chain carriers were made from a steel bar salvaged off a building job. Nylon rollers were machined and fitted to support the chain as it disappears down through the steering head and through the engine room and aft cabin before reappearing on deck via bronze-cased rollers to finally attach to the rudder tiller.

Above left: Repairing the locking mechanism of the steering head.

Above right: Another job done and ready to go back in. The gear within a gypsy gear can be seen.

It was nice to have the old wheel back and during the inspection of our steering gear at the Diamond Jubilee Pageant to see if we were safe to go out on the water, the boat examiner decided we were unlikely to need the emergency steering required on his tick sheet as our steering chains are bigger than most boats' anchor chain.

There have been a whole list of other jobs completed, half completed and thought about. The interior fit-out is nearing completion but since moving onto the boat full time over two years ago, some of the jobs are actually harder to do rather than easier as I am living on her. No one wants to have to do a major clear-up before dinner can go on, or climb into a sawdust-filled bunk.

The engineering jobs have gone well; in fact, anything that involves bolting or screwing new components in place rather than ripping down woodwork or sanding is easy to tackle and complete. A diesel-powered boiler specifically designed for boats runs big double radiators in the saloon and cabins with a much-appreciated large towel rail in the main heads to dry towels.

Right: The helm position protected by the instrument panel.

Below: The instruments and modern navigation equipment.

A Mikuni diesel-powered heating system, which runs domestic hot water and radiators.

Butler sink big enough for all domestic chores.

We also have hot water on tap, which can be heated by the diesel unit or from shore power. There are really good facilities on my home marina so the fit-out of the onboard shower is progressing but there is no rush. I would like to get it finished before the season of maritime festivals, where showers can be in short supply. The main heads boast a posh push-button electric flushing toilet while the forward cabin and crew quarters have good old style hand-pump units, otherwise known as a pump a dump, which are a bit of a mystery to some guests but there is less to go wrong.

Living on board, a well-equipped galley was a must and is fitted with a deep butler sink, which has seen service for all domestic chores from plates and cutlery to bed sheets and even the odd stand-up wash when it's been too cold to walk up to the shower block.

The commercial-size gas hob, oven and grill.

The electric wood-burning stove: very effective without the risk of fire damage to the sails.

Cooking is well covered by a large three-burner gas hob, oven and grill. There is a second electric cooker and of course a microwave.

Food is stored in an upright larder and we have a standard domestic fridge. With modern insulation on fridges and freezers, it easily stays cold enough between unplugging and finding shore power again and cost a fifth of the small and temperamental three-way fridges designed for boats and motorhomes.

I need another session in my woodworking shed to build cabinets that can be fitted in rather than built into the hull, so they can be removed for future maintenance and inspection. It will be an easier way to work than going back to sleeping in a building site as we did for so long.

Left: Lining up with the fleet on the way to the 2015 Dunkirk Return.

Below: In the massive lock at Dunkirk after the crossing from Ramsgate.

We successfully took part in the 2015 Dunkirk Return and for the first time I can actually write that apart from a delayed return crossing due to weather, *Caronia* performed perfectly and we had a fantastic time.

8

The Final Leg

Having completed all the major repairs, the engines, fuel systems and gotten the interior if not finished then at least habitable, there was one job that couldn't be ignored. It couldn't be ignored because every time you looked at *Caronia* it was obvious there was something missing: masts. It really was time for the sticks and rags to go back on.

For many years our only means of flying the dressing overall flags required at events were the somewhat less than classic soil pipe masts. As in, short 3–4 metre, 110 mm diameter domestic soil pipe. It was better than nothing sticking in the sky and it was all we could have carried height-wise when we took part in the 2012 Pageant. If we had been standing our full woodwork we couldn't have got under the bridges and would have missed out on one of the most significant historic events of my lifetime.

There was one slight moment as we sailed from Cannery Warf to our overnight mooring at Barn Elms; there was information provided in hand-outs for our procession back down the Thames the following day, giving water depths and clearance under bridges, but on the way up our plastic flag poles only missed the underside of Tower Bridge by less than 6 inches!

There were no masts for *Caronia* to use as a pattern. When I bought her nearly a decade and a half ago she stood a small mizzen and up in the yard was a motley collection of old mast parts, mostly delaminated lengths of part-rotten timber. For one mad evening I did look at the internet to see if it was even feasible to get masts made and found there are bespoke mast builders with impressive yards and workshops building joinery fit to exhibit in the Tate, let alone adorn the deck of an old fishing boat. But we had done everything else ourselves and it didn't seem right to spend years standing in the wheelhouse looking out on someone else's work adorning the deck.

Considerable research confirmed my original thoughts: that one-piece solid masts would be the way to go. I further researched construction methods, timber use and, not least, the diameter and height. After finding very little on the internet, I don't think the World Wide Web had been dreamt of when adzing and spoke shaving were in regular use.

I turned to old books and, combined with engineering logic, concluded a mast height of approximately 23 feet on the mizzen and 30 feet on the main would work. One of my main 'search tools' was looking at photos of other fishing boat gaffers and scaling the masts off the screen to a known waterline length.

Caronia had deck-mounted tabernacles when I bought her with dimensions to accommodate approximately a 5-inch-square base on the mizzen and a 6-inch-square on the main. The tabernacles had been off during the deck rebuild and had been repaired and hot-dipped galvanised. They were bolted back onto their footplates and ready to accept the long anticipated masts.

It's a long way from Chichester, West Sussex, to Boston, Lincolnshire, but that is what was required to go to the timber yard that supplies poles and pilings for telegraph and mooring jetties. They had agreed to get a selection of 7 and 9-metre light poles off the stack for me to inspect. The light refers to the diameter of the pole; you get light, medium and heavy classes for the same length. I drove up, viewed half a dozen poles of each size in a shed that came straight off the set of *Raiders of the Lost Ark*, then turned around and headed home having paid what in real terms is a lot of money but, if you're talking masts, not a lot for two very straight big lumps of timber.

The mainmast tabernacle bolted back in place after repair and galvanising.

The poles arriving from the timber yard to start their conversion to the new masts.

The poles are Eastern European pine sustainably grown for the industry. They are stored and seasoned to a certain degree before their processing into telegraph, lighting or any other type of pole or piling. They are not, however, joinery timber seasoned, dried and guaranteed to remain free from splits, shakes, warping or cracking.

My plan was to reduce their bulk to allow the timber to further dry at close to its finished size. I had negotiated some space in a boat cover shed in which to undertake the transformation from poles to masts. The open ends helped season the timber with a through draft, although it was a noticeable few degrees colder in the shed than outside in the sun and the draft always seemed to be on the back of your neck!

Both masts would require a square base, which I decided to run up to slightly above wheelhouse height, as until they were actually on the boat the final position of the goosenecks could not be identified. Over the years of the rebuild I had looked at many wooden masts and had found early on that very few round wooden masts are in fact round.

The technique tended to be to start with a round 'tree', turn it into a square blank, mark on the blank guide lines and, having removed that material to form an octagon, mark more guidelines and remove that material to form sixteen sides, then keep on doing that until you have a round form of close to the finished size with many small flat sides to it. Then sand the flats to meet and there is your round tapering mast.

I considered a few ways to start machining the poles into masts and decided to build a guide to router the square onto the base of the main mast. In hindsight it may have been better to try the technique on the smaller mizzen first but I wanted to lighten the main as much as possible so I at least stood half a chance of moving it around the shed.

The router frame used to guide the cutting of the base square on the mainmast.

Above left: Guidelines used to aid the reduction of the poles down to the required size for the masts.

Above right: Planning the square base on the mizzen mast without using the router frame.

I made a frame and lined it onto the pole by a string line and eye. A router was used to gradually reduce the butt end of the pole until the desired square was reached. I was pleasantly surprised as to how easily this was achieved.

That then gave me a long parallel square section to use as a guide to plane down the rest of the pole. With a handheld electric planner, I simply planed and planed, working over about 2 feet at a time with a kind of ironing to-and-fro action. I did put on a few guide lines to work to but found I could work quite well without using the square to octagon to hexadecagon to triacontadigon method.

The pole had a natural taper but nowhere enough to give the final form I wanted. So the first cuts were done with five or six passes of the plane and the next section seven to eight, the next nine to ten, and so on to increase the angle of the taper by removing more material proportionally the closer I got to the top of the mast.

I then left the masts to their own devices for about three weeks in total and they dried out nicely. As expected, they suffered a number of splits, both shallow and deep. The options with the shakes or splits are to fill with a flexible material such as a marine sealant to allow it to move if need be or glue the splits in the hope that the split, once formed, will only go so far and it can be permanently secured with good glue.

I went for the glue option and turned each split upwards and squeezed in modern glue. I like the performance of Gorilla wood glue, which I comfortably believe is not actually made from boiled gorillas unlike the boiled horse hoof glue I can remember my grandad using.

Using a big sander I followed the curve of the wood with an arcing motion, working around the circumference rather than along the length of the mast. It was fairly easy to imagine the round in your mind's eye and keep the sander working that round. I decided to run the round to just above the intended location of the goosenecks and then to an octagon with broad flats and small corners and then to a full square to fit into the tabernacle.

The last wood cutting job was to drill a couple of countersinks into the base of the masts to let in two penny coins. The tradition of placing coins under masts is thousands of years old and there are many theories as to why it's done. The usual belief is that it will bring luck and if it doesn't and your vessel is dismasted, you will have a coin to pay the ferryman to take you to the afterlife. Don't know if a penny would be enough for his fare but if my new mast fell off after all this work I would probably row there myself.

The base of the mizzen, with the penny for luck let in.

The masts after their six coats of Sikens wood treatment.

The main mast button top and flag staff.

I was still undecided as to full high-gloss varnish with all the glory of the wood showing through or some form of preserver, stain and sealer. After applying a thin varnish coat the wood looked very patchy. I therefore went for a stain sealer. Not cheap but six coats of Sikkens light oak have achieved the exact look I wanted. You can still see the wood but it is all blended to an even colour and the sheen rather than gloss is perfect. A couple of button tops and a bit of white paint for the flag staff and they were done!

When it came to the furniture, I had acquired over the years of the rebuild a collection of mast fittings. I had mast bands of a suitable size and had planed the masts to allow the bands to fit very tightly in their required location. Following a trip to the galvanisers, they were driven into their final positions with the aid of ratchet straps and a large hammer. With them on, the masts started to take on a very purposeful look.

 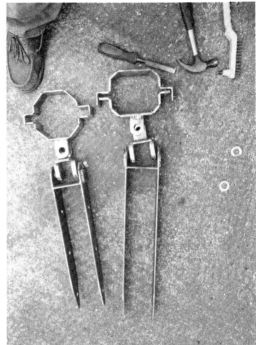

Above left: Welding the gooseneck lugs to allow vertical and horizontal movement.

Above right: The gooseneck awaiting painting or galvanising.

The goosenecks were another matter. Nothing I had or could find suited the shape and requirement of my design. The only option, as usual, was to build from scratch bespoke fabricated metalwork. There are steel stockists around who will supply short lengths of steel, but as so often these days, it was just as easy to order off line. One company could supply all the sizes I wanted in lengths I could handle and I could sit in the comfort of my wheelhouse and order everything for two-day delivery. I cut, shaped and arc welded the clamps and plates and boom fittings in my metalworking shed; it's the same as the woodwork shed, just a different range of tools.

The last leg before the masts were stepped was sorting the rigging, which, being a fishing boat, is galvanised. A very successful day at Beaulieu had sourced all the tufnol pulleys that would be required at a bargain price. As with the masts, I had spent hours looking at other gaff rigs, taken many photographs and read many books. I think the conclusion I came to was that there are as many standing rigging configurations as there are boats on the sea.

I went for engineering logic and the principle that if it looks right, it probably is. The chain plates had been made, hot-dipped galvanised and bolted on some weeks previously.

I booked a slot under the mast crane and moved *Caronia* over. On the day I decided to enlist the help of the onsite rigging company and let them swage the wires using my materials. It was a long day and took two of their guys, myself and my son, but by the end of the day the new masts were on deck and for the first time in years *Caronia* looked like a fishing boat again rather than a barge.

Flying the dressing overall flags at the local Birdham classic weekend.

The first time in a very long time: sails up and looking like a boat again.

The next week or three saw the goosenecks, booms, synthetic hemp rigging and, best bargain of all, the sails go on.

On the way to our participation in the filming of *Dunkirk* (the cover picture) we managed to get the mizzen steadying sail up. The difference it made was remarkable and steadying is exactly what it did. The wind, as people with sticks and rags tell me is usual, was against us for the rest of the trip so she is as yet to be adorned with mizzen, main and head sail in the breeze, although we did get the dressing overall flags up at a classic event back at our old home of Birdham Pool, the first time we've had enough woodwork to fly the full set!

Of all the jobs completed on *Caronia*, building the masts and seeing her rerigged has got to be one of the most satisfying. I think it probably took more thinking about and a fair bit of research to source all the materials than actual work itself.

9

The Future

Some people think I am mad for the amount of time and effort I have put into restoring *Caronia* and I know there are still things to finish and maintenance will never stop but I think I really have reached the end of the major works and projects now. We have a well-equipped, sound and capable vessel. Besides, if I actually finish everything on *Caronia*, what would I do next?

We can now do with *Caronia* everything we always wanted to. Summer cruises to historic and picturesque harbours and ports. This year (2017) we appear in the Warner Brothers release *Dunkirk*.

We have the great honour this year of flying the National Historic Flagship of the Year pennant, having received the prestigious award this June at the Yarmouth Old Gaffers.

The award really is recognition of all the years of restoration and our commitment to the maritime heritage of our seafaring nation and we couldn't be prouder of *Caronia*. The work may continue but so does the history and adventures with my family.

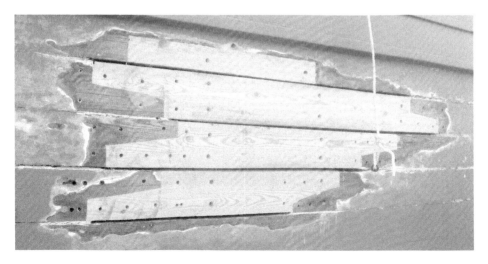

Some further hull repairs done in 2013.

Left: The incredible
amount of wiring even
a simple instrument
panel needs.

Below: Preparing the
coach roof for the new
cover with a waterproof
base layer.

On set at the filming of *Dunkirk* – a motley looking crew.

A few extras on deck. We had twenty and could have taken many times that number.

Above: Leaving Dunkirk harbour to film with other Little Ships.

Left: The skipper at the helm, looking like an advert for sardines.

Right: Lewis and Wilson in 2010 on the way back from Ramsgate.

Below: Natalie and Wilson on the way back from the filming in Dunkirk in 2016. It took a long time to match the one of Lewis due to Natalie's four years at university.

All of us in Yarmouth at the presentation of the National Historic Ships Broad Pennant as flagship of the year for the Solent.

In the weeks since this book went off to the publishers for its first layout, the life and adventures with *Caronia* have continued. Maybe for the pages of another volume is the log of the voyage I have just completed single-handed – well, single-crewed with the able assistance of Wilson as always. I spent the early summer taking *Caronia* back to the beach where she was built so long ago. We visited many harbours along the way: Gosport, Yarmouth, Weymouth, Torquay, Dartmouth, Plymouth, Falmouth, Penzance and finally Newlyn to collect a small pot of sand from the beach were her keel was laid.

The release of the Warner Brothers *Dunkirk* film saw Natalie and I attending the red carpet premier in London. I said to her as the film started, 'How did acquiring an old wooden boat get us to this point?' I think the Father's Day card Natalie and Lewis gave me this year simple sums it all up; along with the generic printed Father's Day wishes Natalie had written: 'Thank you for all our adventures, Natalie and Lewis.'